Half Yard Kids

Sew 20 colourful toys and accessories from left-over pieces of fabric

Debbie Shore

SEARCH PRESS

First published in 2016

Search Press Limited
Wellwood, North Farm Road,
Tunbridge Wells, Kent TN2 3DR

Photographs by Garie Hind
Styling by Kimberley Hind

ISBN: 978-1-78221-255-3

For further inspiration, visit Debbie's website:
www.debbieshore.tv

Suppliers
For details of suppliers, please visit the
Search Press website: www.searchpress.com

Printed in China

Dedication

This book just has to be dedicated to my
kids, David, Kimberley and Tyler, who
continue to make me the proudest mum
(and grandma!) as they grow into their
twenties and thirties. When they were
small, I made them dressing-up outfits
and costumes for school plays and ballet
classes. There were also many repairs
to split seams and patches over worn-
out knees, and bespoke toys, teddies
and even wrestling buddies that you just
can't buy in the shops! Now they are
all grown up, it is mainly curtains and
cushions with the occasional mending
job to a tear in a jacket or a hole in a
pocket... but I must admit we all played
monkey skittles and fished for fish as I
was working on this book!

Acknowledgements

Thanks to the kids who put my
projects to the test: Ella-Mei, Mia, Poppy,
Oliver, Evie, Rebecca and Harry.

To my husband Garie who's responsible
for the amazing photography, and the
Search Press team for giving me such a
fun book to work on!

Half Yard

Kids

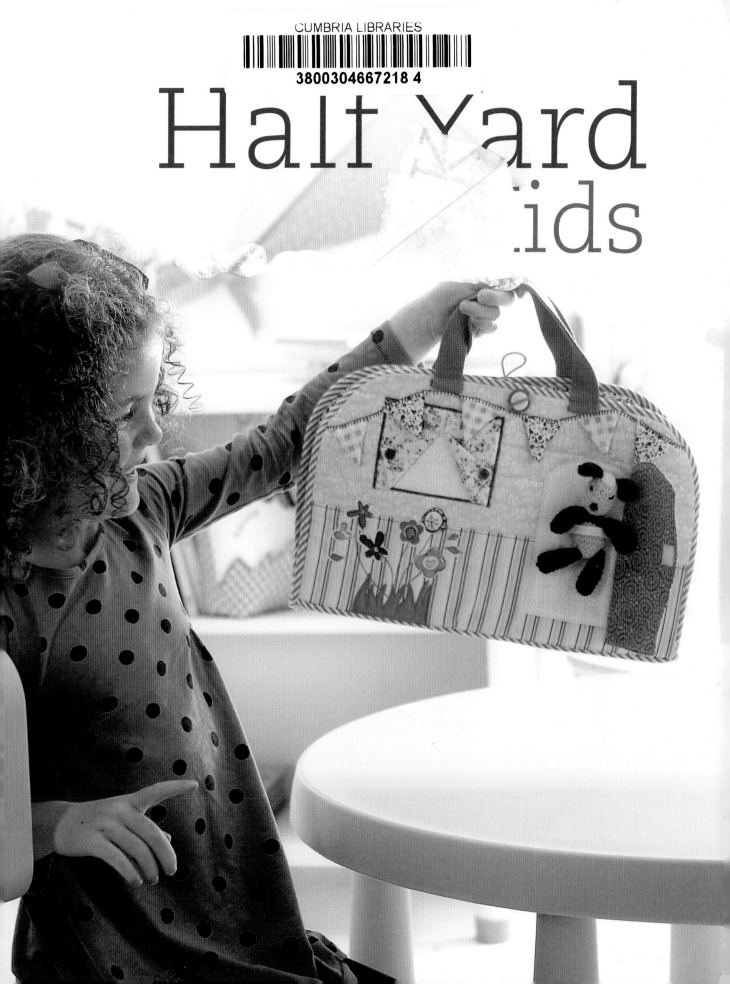

Contents

Craft easel,
page 16

Fish for fish, ditch the crab!,
page 22

Monkey skittles,
page 44

Hot water bottle,
page 48

Patchwork ball,
page 52

Porthole curtains,
page 70

Pyjama eater,
page 72

Shoe bag,
page 76

Roaring storing!,
page 78

Foxy drawing folder,
page 28

Halloween bunting,
page 34

Crafty kids' backpack,
page 36

Witch's hat,
page 54

Pillow pal,
page 58

Cube tidy,
page 64

Chair pockets,
page 66

Kite wall hanging,
page 82

Caravan caddy,
page 84

Miss Monster bookend,
page 90

Coin purse
page 94

Introduction

I've had so much fun making up the projects in this book, and I'm sure the kids will enjoy using and playing with them too! I've included something for all ages, from dressing-up Halloween hats and monkey skittles to pirate cuddle pillows and useful storage solutions, all with simple-to-understand instructions. There are hints and tips throughout, and hopefully you'll be able to use the techniques like zip insertion and applying bias binding for future projects.

I like to use 100 per cent woven cotton for most of the projects: quilting cotton comes in so many lovely prints and colours, and if you need to add a bit more rigidity to the fabric then simply back it with wadding (batting). I use 40 per cent wool felt – I find this stronger than 100 per cent wool felt. It can be stuffed tightly without stretching but still feels soft to the touch (as with the patchwork ball, see pages 52–53). I use a ¼in (5mm) seam allowance unless otherwise stated.

Debbie x

Useful things

FABRICS

Choosing your fabric wisely is so important – a quality fabric will last well, is a pleasure to work with and will produce a quality project. I've used 100 per cent cotton fabric for most of the projects in this book, and felt for a few of the others. I prefer a wool mixed felt – look for at least 40 per cent wool; although pure wool felt feels wonderfully soft, it's not as strong as a wool mixed with synthetic material. Synthetic or craft felts tend to be a little stiff and scratchy, so avoid these if you can.

RIBBONS

Ribbon adds that finishing touch to a project, whether it is in the form of a bow or a border. I like to keep a variety of colours and widths in my stash, as they always come in useful.

THREADS

Choose your thread as carefully as you choose your fabric: good-quality thread is strong and will produce less lint build-up in your sewing machine. Try to match the fibre content with the type of fabric you're using – for example, cotton for cotton, and polyester for synthetics.

BUTTONS

Not just for fastenings, buttons can hide the odd wobbly stitch or stain or just add extra detail when used as embellishments. I like the look of two or even three buttons of different sizes and colours layered on top of one another. To make them a bit more secure, pop a little strong clear fabric glue behind them.

BAMBOO CREASER

Use this tool for creasing seams and pushing out the points of your projects when you turn them right side out. It's not so sharp that it will pierce your fabric, and for pressing small seams it's quicker than putting on the iron!

ERASABLE INK PENS

Erasable ink is either heat-, air- or water-erasable. Heat-erasable types will disappear with friction or heat from your iron (this is my preference), water-erasable types will disappear when dampened and air-erasable types will disappear after a few hours. Be aware that water- and air-erasable inks will become permanent if ironed, so choose carefully!

SCISSORS

I find it handy to keep a selection: have one pair for fabric, one for paper, and one small pair for snipping threads.

APPLIQUÉ SCISSORS

If your stitching isn't quite perfect and you need to trim away a part of your appliqué, these duck-billed scissors will enable you to trim the appliqué piece without cutting through the main fabric. They also tend to be sharp right to the top, so are perfect for snipping threads and cutting into curves.

FABRIC CLIPS

For when pins just aren't strong enough, or if you are using fabrics that you don't want to puncture, such as vinyls or oilcloths, use these mini clips to hold your work together before sewing.

ADHESIVES

Repositionable spray adhesive is useful for holding down appliqué pieces without pins; use it also to hold layers of fabric together while sewing. Permanent spray adhesive is activated by the heat from your iron and is a good way to fuse wadding (batting) to your fabric. Make sure any adhesives you use are suitable for fabric so as not to damage your machine. A strong, clear fabric glue is an alternative to stitching in some instances.

SEWING MACHINE

You don't need many stitches: straight and zigzag are useful, and a buttonhole stitch is handy too. A free arm is invaluable when top-stitching around the opening of a bag or pouch, and the option to have the needle stop in the 'down' position is helpful when sewing around corners. Change your needle regularly, and use a strong needle for thick fabrics.

TWEEZERS

You will find tweezers really useful for picking up small items such as googly eyes and buttons, and also for holding onto small pieces of fabric that you are glueing, to keep your fingers from getting sticky!

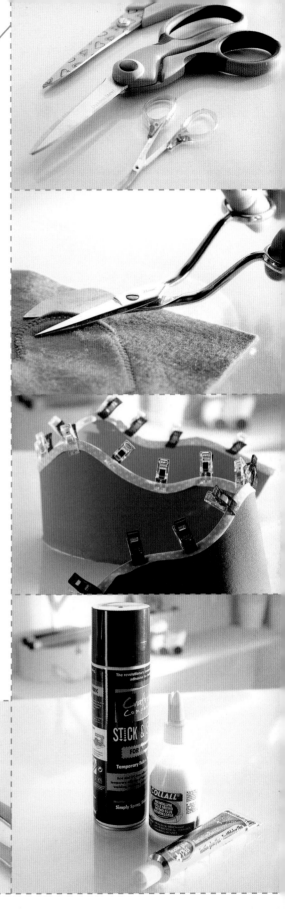

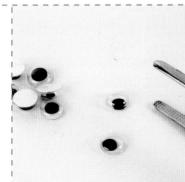

Before you start

- Many fabrics nowadays are pre-shrunk, but if you're not sure, wash and dry your fabric before cutting it.
- Take your time measuring and cutting fabric. If your stitching is wrong, you can always unpick, but if you cut your fabric wrong, it could cost you more fabric.
- If you're not too good at sewing in a straight line, put a piece of tape over the flat bed of your sewing machine to use as a guide.
- Always use good-quality thread. There's a time and place for saving money, but don't skimp when it comes to thread! Cheap thread can break easily and shed fibres into your sewing machine.
- Change your machine needle after about eight hours of sewing; a blunt needle can pucker your fabric.

- Good lighting is essential for successful sewing. Daylight bulbs allow you to see the true colours.
- Ironing is an important part of sewing. Your seams will sit better and you'll have a more professional finish if you iron them as you go. Pre-ironed fabric is easier to work with.
- Always use sharp scissors, and never use your fabric scissors to cut paper as it will blunt them.
- The seam allowance is the distance sewn from the edge of the fabric. For the projects in this book I've allowed ¼in (5mm) unless stated otherwise.

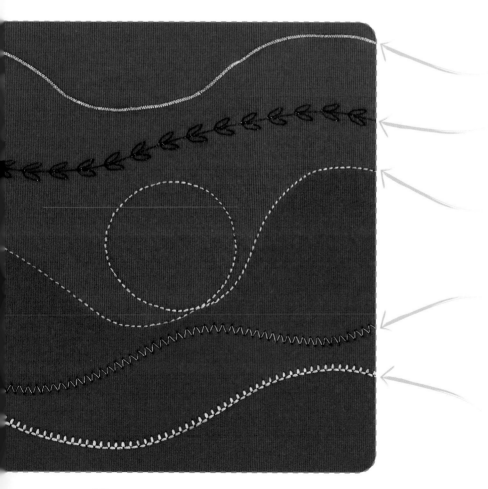

MACHINE STITCHES

Satin stitch: a short zigzag stitch that is used for decoration or sewing appliqué.

Decorative stitch: many sewing machines have a variety of built-in decorative stitches. These add pretty top-stitches to personalise your projects.

Triple straight stitch: this stitch is usually used for stretch fabrics, but it can also be used as a top-stitch and gives a bold straight line.

Zigzag: even if your sewing machine is quite basic it should have a zigzag stitch. This useful stitch helps to prevent the raw edges of woven fabric fraying, but as a decorative stitch it also looks particularly good on felt.

Blanket stitch: I use this a lot for appliqué: it binds the fraying edge of your fabric and gives a hand-stitched look to your work.

HAND STITCHES

Running stitch: take the needle in and out of the fabric at even intervals. A running stitch creates a hand-made look when used as a top-stitch. If used instead of a sewing machine for seams, make the stitch as small as you can.

Blanket stitch: if you're hand sewing appliqué, particularly in felt, this traditional blanket stitch creates a neat outline. Keep your stitches uniform, ¼in (5mm) wide and long.

Backstitch: use either side of the stitch to create a straight line – particularly useful when embroidering features on a face.

Cross stitch: I like to make the stitches slightly different in length, and a random scattering of cross stitches adds interest to plain fabric where a patterned fabric wouldn't work.

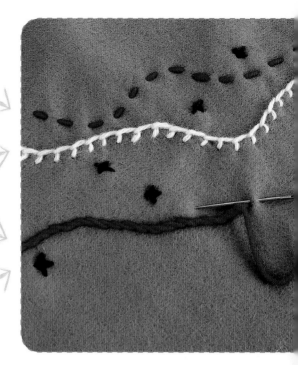

Using a continuous zip

Always use your zipper foot when fitting a zip, as it allows you to sew close to the coil or teeth. A nylon zip that is too long can simply be cut down to the right size, but I prefer to use continuous zipping, which can be cut to any length you require.

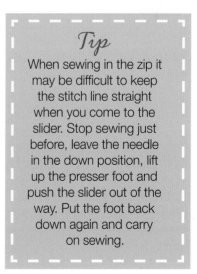

1 To fit the slider to a continuous zip, open up the end of the zip. Cut along the coil of one side by about ½in (1cm). Cut off the other side at this point.

2 Slide the tab over the exposed coil, then over the opposite side of the zip, and gently pull until both sides of the coil engage. Don't worry if the zip looks uneven; open and close the zip a couple of times and it will right itself.

Tip

When sewing in the zip it may be difficult to keep the stitch line straight when you come to the slider. Stop sewing just before, leave the needle in the down position, lift up the presser foot and push the slider out of the way. Put the foot back down again and carry on sewing.

Making a square base

I have used this technique to square off the bottom of my Miss Monster bookend project (see pages 90–93), but it is also a very handy technique to have up your sleeve if you are making bags or pouches.

1 First, fold the bottom seam over the side seam and pin. Make sure the seams are lined up – you can feel the seams through the fabric.

2 Measure from the point, across the bottom seam according to the instructions for your project, and mark with a pencil. Sew across this line, back-tacking at each end of the stitch line.

3 Cut away the corners of the fabric.

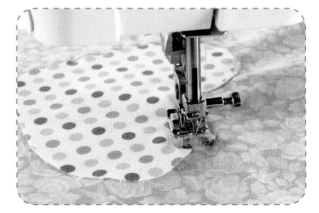

4 When turned, the corners should look like this.

Appliqué

Set your sewing machine to a wide zigzag stitch and test on a piece of scrap fabric – you may prefer a narrower stitch. Centre the edge of the shape under the middle of your satin-stitch foot, and gently guide it under the foot. Don't push or pull as the fabric will distort. Stitch all the way around the shape.

A satin-stitch foot has two ski-like bars underneath that raise the foot up slightly, allowing the dense stitches to pass underneath easily.

Making bias binding

Bias tape is a strip of fabric cut on the diagonal, at a 45-degree angle. Cutting on the bias allows a little 'give', so the fabric will stretch around curves without puckering. To make bias binding you will need to fold over both long edges of the tape into the centre and press. The easiest way to do this is to use either a bias binding machine or a small bias tape maker (shown), through which you thread the tape. The tape maker folds the strip in two – you press with your iron while pulling the fabric through.

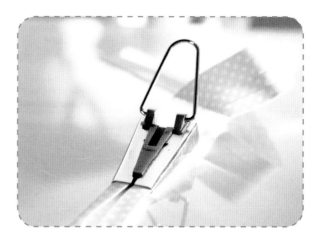

Applying bias binding

1 To apply the binding, first open up the crease lines and fold over the end: crease this with your fingers. Right sides together, pin along the raw edge of your work. Sew with your machine along the crease mark, all the way around your project, and when you come back to the beginning, overlap the binding by about ½in (1cm).

2 Now fold the tape over the raw edge, and use a slip stitch to sew by hand on the back of the piece. An alternative is to top-stitch from the front with your machine, but bear in mind that these stitches will be seen so you'll need to sew a really straight line! If the binding is attached around a curve it will stretch easily.

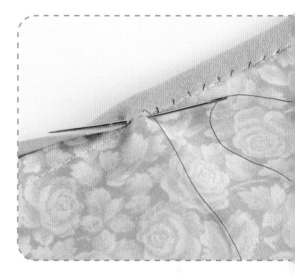

Cutting into curves

For curves that are to be turned, make little 'V'-shaped cuts into the fabric up to the seam – this will stop the fabric from puckering when turned. You could also use pinking shears for the same effect.

Cutting corners

This helps to keep the corners square when turned the right way out; cut away the corner, keeping as close to the stitches as you can, without snipping them.

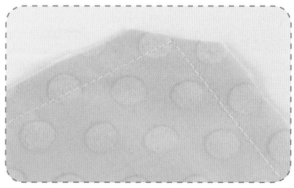

Craft easel

This is a handy storage unit for the crafter or little artist, which folds flat to make it easy to carry. It can easily be adapted to make it larger or smaller, and you can always add a few more pockets if you need them.

1 For the front of the easel, take one large piece of fabric, four of the 6in (15.25cm) pocket pieces (two pairs of different fabrics) and two 3in (7.5cm) pocket pieces. You'll notice these are slightly wider than the mountboard.

What you need

Two pieces of mountboard or stiff card, measuring 9½ x 12in (24 x 30cm)

Four pieces of fabric to cover, measuring 10¼in (26cm) wide by 13in (33cm) long

For the pockets, six pieces of fabric (four from one fabric, two from another) measuring 10¼ x 6in (26 x 15.25cm), and four pieces measuring 10¼ x 3in (26 x 7.5cm)

For the base, two pieces of fabric measuring 10¼ x 8in (26 x 20.5cm)

90in (229cm) of 1in (2.5cm) wide bias binding

16in (40.5cm) elastic

Two elastic hair bands

Two large buttons for stoppers

Four smaller buttons to fasten: I like to use a small button on top of a large one

Embroidery thread

Clear fabric glue

Erasable ink pen

Bamboo creaser

2 Place the pocket pieces in pairs, right sides together, and sew across the bottom edges.

3 Fold each pocket over to the right side, and press in half. Sew a length of bias binding to the top of each pocket (see page 15).

4 Measure 4in (10cm) from the bottom of the large piece of fabric, pin one 6in (15.25cm) pocket so that its bottom edge aligns at this point and sew across the bottom.

5 Measure 2in (5cm) from the bottom. Place the second 6in (15.25cm) pocket over the first, so that its bottom edge aligns at this point, and sew across the bottom.

6 Repeat with the final 3in (7.5cm) pocket, aligning its bottom edge 1½in (4cm) from the bottom.

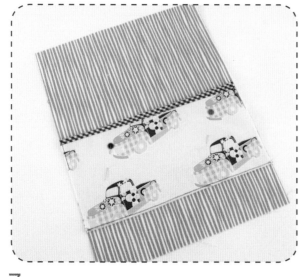

7 For the back of the easel, take the remaining four pocket pieces (two large and two small) and make two pockets from them in the same way as in steps 2 and 3.

8 Position the 6in (15.25cm) pocket on the other large piece of fabric, 2in (5cm) from the bottom. Sew across the bottom of the pocket.

9 The 3in (7.5cm) pocket is then placed 1½in (4cm) from the bottom of the fabric, overlapping the first pocket – sew it across the bottom.

10 Draw a line with an erasable ink pen 3in (7.5cm) from the top of the fabric – this is where the elastic will go. Starting at one side, sew the elastic in place at 1in (2.5cm) intervals, looping it slightly between stitches to form pockets that will accommodate pencils.

11 If you have any extra elastic when you come to the other side, trim away with scissors.

12 Lay down the front and back panels with the top ends together, and join with a strip of bias tape – stitch along each side of the bias tape.

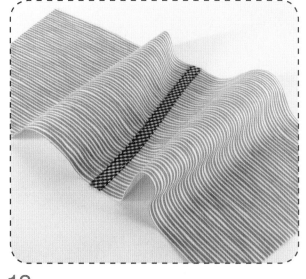

13 You still have two large pieces of fabric remaining: join these together with bias tape in the same way as in step 12.

14 Place these two pieces together, right sides facing. Sew together along the long sides to make a tube, making sure the bias tape lines up in the middle. Turn the tube right side out and press. Sew straight along the middle of the bias tape join.

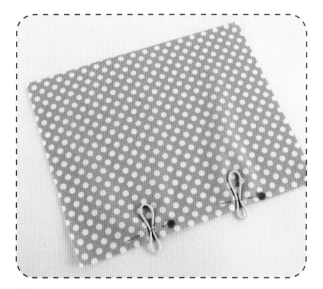

15 Push one piece of mountboard inside the back of the easel. It should fit snugly!

16 To make the base, mark the centre point of one of the longer sides of the fabric by folding in half and creasing it, then measure 2½in (5cm) each side of this point. Pin the hair bands at these points, on the right side of the fabric, facing inwards.

17 Tack (baste) the hair bands in place. Sew the two base pieces right sides together, leaving the side opposite the hair bands open.

18 Snip across the corners and turn right side out. Use a bamboo creaser to push out the points.

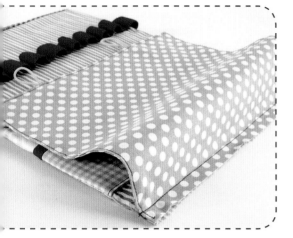

19 Press, then top-stitch. Sew the base to the bottom of the right side of the back easel piece, underneath the mountboard. You may wish to use a zipper foot to take the needle closer to the board.

20 Apply bias binding to cover the raw edge, folding the ends inwards to make neat. I found it easier to sew the tape as it's folded over by hand.

21 Fold the easel in half with the pockets facing each other. Fold over the base panel, not too tightly, and mark where the hair bands sit.

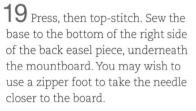

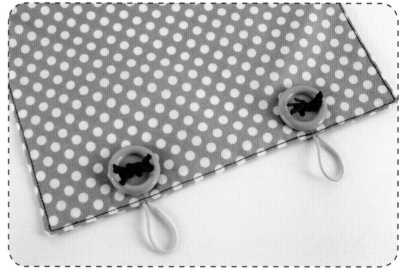

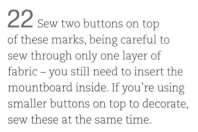

22 Sew two buttons on top of these marks, being careful to sew through only one layer of fabric – you still need to insert the mountboard inside. If you're using smaller buttons on top to decorate, sew these at the same time.

23 Push the remaining piece of mountboard inside this sleeve, sew the bottom closed, then apply bias binding over the edge.

24 Finally, take the two large buttons, and sew embroidery thread through the holes, I've knotted mine on the front of the button. Glue these in place on the base of the easel, just above the elastic hair bands. To make sure you have them on the correct side, stand the easel up with the pockets on the outside, and place the buttons at the front of the base fabric to act as stoppers.

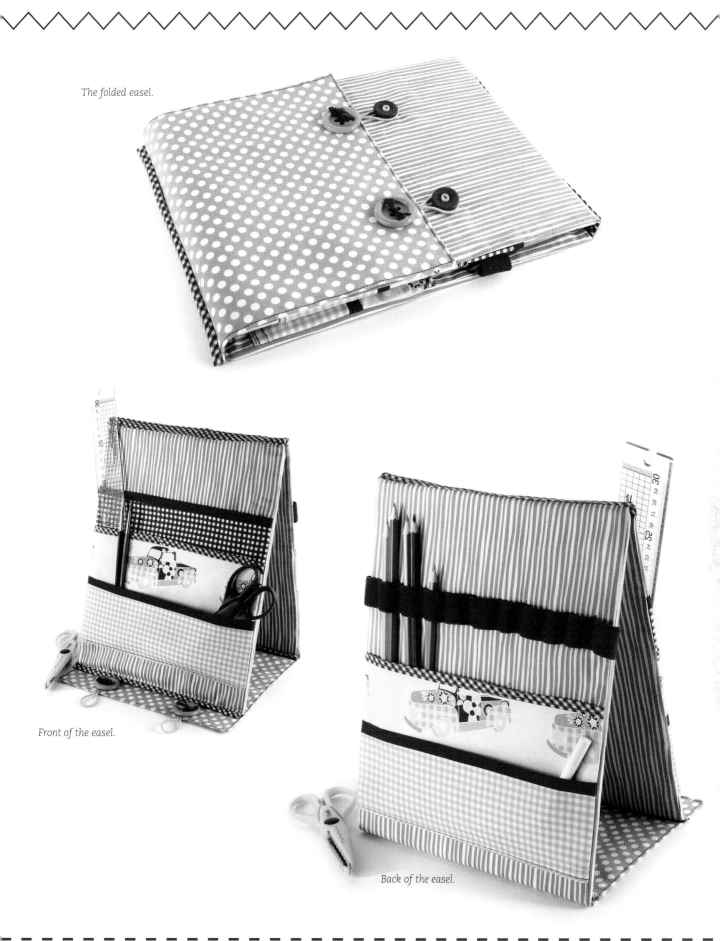

The folded easel.

Front of the easel.

Back of the easel.

Fish for fish, ditch the crab!

Have fun with the kids catching these cute little fish in their own tank! Try putting numbers or initials on the backs of the fish to make the game a little more difficult. The idea here is that you catch the fish, not the crabs, but they all have magnets in their noses, so you have to be careful!

1 First let's make the fish. For each one, cut a piece of fabric measuring 5 x 5in (13 x 13cm), and a piece of contrasting fabric measuring 5 x 2½in (13 x 6.5cm).

2 The fins are made from a 2in (5cm) circle of fabric, cut into quarters. Use two per fish. Place the fins, facing inwards, 1¾in (4.5cm) from either side, as shown.

3 Place the smaller contrasting strip of fabric right sides together over the top of the larger piece, and sew. Open up and press, then top-stitch to look neat. The smaller section of fabric will be the head.

What you need

For four fish:
Two pieces of contrasting fabric measuring 5 x 20in (13 x 51cm)
One felt square for the fins
A 2in (5cm) round template
Eight googly eyes
Toy filling
Strong thread
Four small strong magnets
Strong fabric glue

For two crabs:
Two strips of orange fabric – one plain, one spot – each 10 x 4in (25.5 x 10cm)
Four googly eyes
A 5in (13cm) square of orange felt for the legs
Toy filling
Two small strong magnets
A 4in (10cm) round template

For the rod:
Two small strong magnets
Embroidery thread or string
A stick, or piece of dowelling

For the tank:
30 x 10in (76.25 x 25.5cm) piece of clear vinyl
Two 10in (25.5cm) circles of blue fabric
10in (25.5cm) circle of foam stabiliser
Spray fabric adhesive
Two 30 x 3in (76.25 x 7.5cm) pieces of blue fabric
30 x 3in (76.25 x 7.5cm) piece of firm stabiliser
125in (317.5cm) of 1in (2.5cm) wide bias binding
A few shells
Clear fabric glue
Fabric clips

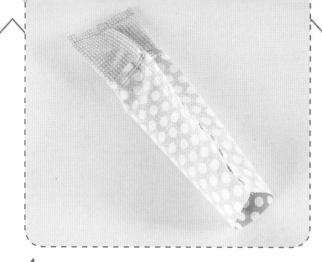

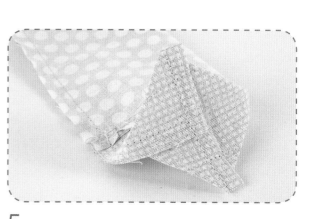

4 Fold the two long sides right sides together and sew into a tube. Manipulate so that the seam lies in the centre, then sew across the head end.

5 Pull open the fabric either side of the seam to form a square shape, then sew over the top and bottom of this seam, ½in (1cm) from each point. This will make the nose of the fish square.

6 Turn your fish right side out. Carefully drop one of the small magnets into the nose, then stuff about two-thirds full with toy filler.

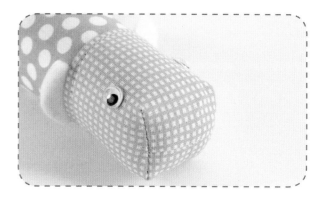

7 Fold the open end of the fish inwards by ¼in (5mm) and press. Sew across the opening.

8 Take some strong thread and tie around the end of the fish – about 1in (2.5cm) from the end – to make a tail, then stick on the eyes with strong fabric glue. If you have concerns about using stick-on eyes with young children, sew buttons for eyes instead.

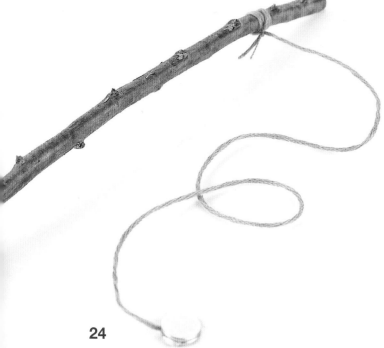

9 To make the fishing line, place two magnets together with the end of your embroidery thread in between. They should be strong enough to hold, but if not, secure them with a dot of strong glue.

10 Tie the other end of the thread around the stick.

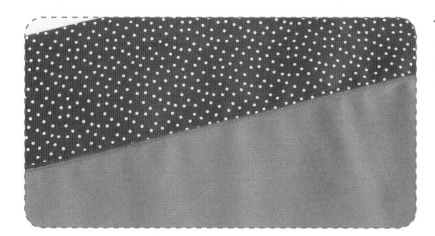

11 Now for the crabs. For each crab, sew together the strip of spot fabric to the plain, press the seam and top-stitch.

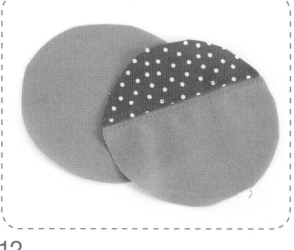

12 Using your round template, cut one circle over the seam, then one from plain fabric.

13 For the legs, cut six pieces of felt, ½ x 2in (1 x 5cm) each, and round off one end of each. The large claws are a 'comma' shape, measuring 2½in (6cm) in length. Place three legs and a claw facing inwards on each side of the circle, with the spot fabric to the top. Tack (baste) them all in place.

14 Place the plain circle on top, and sew all the way round, leaving a gap in the bottom of about 2in (5cm) for turning.

15 Turn right side out, stuff with toy filler and hand-sew the opening closed. Glue on the googly eyes (or sew on buttons). Cut a little 'v' shape into each front claw to give him pincers!

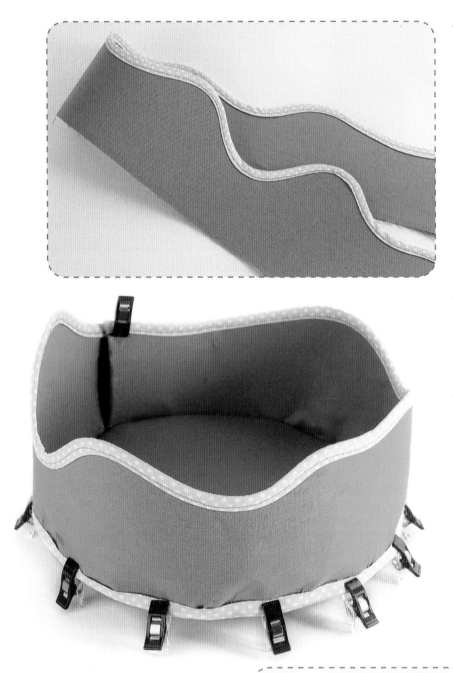

16 Now for the tank. Adhere the two fabric strips to either side of the stabiliser. Cut a wavy line across the top, then apply bias tape along the waves. The easiest way to do this is to iron the bias tape in half lengthways, fold it around the fabric, clip together then sew.

17 Adhere the two fabric circles to either side of the foam stabiliser. Clip and then sew the wavy strip around the edge of the circle, overlapping the ends.

18 Apply bias tape around the raw edge; this time, use fabric glue, it's so much easier than sewing! The trick is to glue one side at a time, and use your clips to hold in place while the glue dries. Glue the ends of the overlapping wavy section together.

19 When the glue is dry, turn the tank inside out.

20 Sew a strip of bias tape to one long edge of the clear vinyl – this will be the top edge.

21 Wrap the clear vinyl strip around the inside of the 'tank', and glue in place.

22 Pop a few shells inside, glue in place if you like, and add a few more around the outside of the tank. Now, anyone for fishing?

Foxy drawing folder

This is a great way to keep pencils, pens and paper organised, and it features a clever pocket on the front with Mr Fox peeping over the top!

Tip

Measure the fabric against a pad to make sure your sizes are right.

What you need

One piece of outer fabric measuring 22 x 12in (56 x 30.5cm)

One piece of lining measuring 22 x 12in (56 x 30.5cm)

One piece of fusible fleece measuring 22 x 12in (56 x 30.5cm)

13in (33cm) red elastic

13in (33cm) blue elastic: I found some with rubber dots on one side, so it grips pens and pencils well

34in (86.5cm) length of continuous zip

The spine pocket is a strip of fabric measuring 8 x 3in (20.5 x 7.5cm)

The front pocket is made of two pieces of fabric each measuring 8 x 5½in (20.5 x 14cm)

The inside pocket is made of two pieces of fabric each measuring 6 x 9in (15.25 x 23cm)

The handles are two strips of fabric each measuring 3 x 12in (7.5 x 30.5cm)

The fox face and paws are made from two pieces of fabric, each measuring 7in (18cm) square

One 7in (18cm) square of fusible fleece

Scraps of black felt

A pair of googly eyes

2in (5cm) of hook and loop fastening

A piece of cardboard measuring 11 x 9in (28 x 23cm)

Four buttons

Fabric glue

Embroidery thread and large needle for sewing the whiskers and paws and for sewing on the buttons

1 First, iron the 7in (18cm) fusible fleece piece to the back of the 7in (18cm) square fox face fabric piece. Cut two equilateral triangles from the foxy face fabric measuring 6½in (16.5cm) on each side.

2 Cut a curve from one point to the other – on both triangles – to make the ears on the top of the head.

3 Glue a triangle of black felt to the bottom point to form a nose. Cut two small felt circles for eyes and glue in place 3in (7.5cm) up from the bottom.

4 Glue the googly eyes on top of the felt circles.

5 On the second triangle, sew one side of the hook and loop fastening across the nose point 1in (2.5cm) from the bottom point. Trim off the overlap.

6 Sew both triangles, right sides together, leaving a gap in one side for turning.

7 Turn right side out and press. Sew closed the opening by hand with a ladder stitch. Hand sew three whiskers to each side of the nose, 2in (5cm) from the point.

8 Cut two circles measuring about 2in (5cm) across, then cut each in half to make four semi-circles for the paws.

9 Pair the semi-circles up, right sides together, and sew around the curved sides only. Turn right side out and press.

10 For the spine pocket, fold each side of the fabric over by about ½in (1cm) and press.

11 Top-stitch across the top edge.

12 Pin in place on the bottom centre edge of the outer fabric, then top-stitch around the bottom three sides (as shown, left).

13 To make up the front pocket, sew the tops of the two pocket pieces together, sandwiching the paws in between, as shown. Sew a 1in (2.5cm) piece of hook and loop fastening centrally, 2in (5cm) from the top of the pocket.

14 With the pocket pieces right sides facing again, sew the sides together.

15 Turn the right way out and press. Fold the open edge inwards by about ½in (1cm) and press.

16 Pin the pocket to the centre bottom front of the case, then sew around the three bottom sides. Sew three toes to each paw with embroidery thread, taking the thread through the pocket fabric only to hold the paws in place.

17 Pop the fox face in place, so that the hook and loop fastenings meet, and sew across the top.

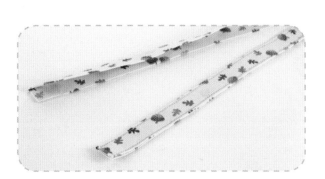

18 For the handles, fold each strip of fabric in half lengthways and press. Fold each raw edge to this centre crease and press again. Tuck in the ends by about ½in (1cm). Fold in half and press again. Top-stitch all the way around.

19 Sew the handles centrally, either side of the spine – position each end about 3in (7.5cm) from the top and bottom. Add the buttons to cover the ends.

20 Round off the corners of each cover piece, both inner and outer. With about 2in (5cm) spare at each end, sew one half of the zip to the front of the outer case, the other to the back of the outer case. Pin the ends of the zip inwards to keep them out of the way.

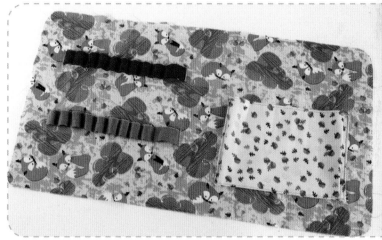

21 Centrally, on the left-hand side of the lining fabric, draw two straight lines, each about 8in (20.5cm) long, where the elastic will sit. Position the top one 3in (7.5cm) from the top of the case and the bottom one 4in (10cm) below the first (see right for guidance).

22 Satin stitch the left-hand end of each piece of elastic in place, then push a pencil up to this stitch line, and using your zipper foot, sew the elastic alongside the pencil. Don't pull the elastic as this will pucker the fabric. Continue until you reach the end. Satin stitch the opposite end of the elastic in place.

23 For the inside pocket, sew the two pieces of fabric right sides together, leaving the bottom open.

24 Turn right side out, fold the opening inwards by about ½in (1cm) and press.

25 Place the pocket centrally on the right-hand half of the lining fabric, 2in (5cm) up from the bottom. Pin the pocket in place, making a little pleat at either side of the bottom edge to form a gusset.

26 Attach by sewing around the sides and bottom edge, sewing over the little pleats as you go.

27 Right sides together, sew the outer panel to the inner, leaving a gap in the bottom of the right-hand side for turning.

28 Turn right side out and press. Be careful of those pins!

29 Feed the cardboard into the opening,

30 Hand-sew the opening closed.

31 Attach the slider to the zip, see page 13.

32 Make two small pouches from left-over fabric to cover each end of the zip, by cutting two rectangles measuring 1½ x 3in (4 x 7.5cm). Fold each in half right sides together, and sew along the two short sides. Turn right side out, and fold the raw edge inwards by ¼in (5mm).

33 Pop a pouch over each zip end, and sew all the way around to complete.

Tip

You could add as many pockets as you like, and adjust the size to fit a favourite colouring book.

Halloween bunting

Felt is such an easy fabric to work with as it doesn't fray so therefore doesn't need hemming. I enjoyed experimenting with the facial expressions here – some of my pumpkin pennants look happy, some quite scary and some a little bit worried!

What you need

For each pennant, a triangle of orange felt measuring 6in (15.25cm) across by 9in (23cm) deep

Scraps of black felt for the features

1in (2.5cm) wide bias tape, as long as you'd like the bunting to be!

Fabric glue

Tip
Try making the bunting in white felt to create scary ghosts!

1 Cut out the number of triangles needed: you'll fit four to 1 yard (91.5cm) of bias tape, leaving a little tape at each end to tie.

2 Cut a wavy edge along the two long sides.

3 For the face, cut two black felt triangles about 1½in (4cm) across, then cut a small arc in the bottom of the triangle to create eyes. The nose is a smaller triangle, and the mouth is a crescent shape, with a few notches cut out for teeth!

4 Try to make each face a little different: perhaps add eyebrows or a wavy line for a mouth, or try turning the triangle eyes upside down. When you're happy with the result, glue the pieces in place.

5 Fold the bias tape in half lengthways and press.

6 Wrap this around the top edges of the halloween pennants and pin, leaving 5in (13cm) or so at each end for tying. Sew in place with a zigzag stitch on your machine.

Crafty kids' backpack

This backpack is the perfect school bag, with a zipped inside pocket and storage for pens behind the flap on the front. I like to use a continuous zip that I can cut to size: guidance for attaching a slider is given on page 13. With this method of zipping, you could attach two sliders so that the zip closes in the centre.

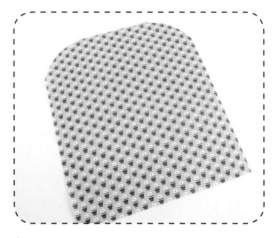

1 Take the two outer and two lining pieces of fabric and using the plate as a template, mark then cut the top two corners into curves. Iron fusible fleece to the wrong side of the outer fabric pieces.

What you need

Two pieces of outer fabric measuring 12in (30.5cm) wide by 14in (35.5cm) long

Two pieces of lining fabric measuring 12in (30.5cm) wide by 14in (35.5cm) long

Two pieces of fusible fleece measuring 12 x 14in (30.5 x 35.5cm)

For the zipped panel, four pieces of fabric measuring 29 x 2½in (73.75 x 6.5cm)

Two pieces of fusible fleece measuring 29 x 2½in (73.75 x 6.5cm)

30in (76.25cm) zip

Four pieces of fabric measuring 5in (13cm) wide by 4½in (11.5cm) long

Two pieces of fusible fleece measuring 4½ x 5in (11.5 x 13cm)

For the inside pocket, two pieces of fabric measuring 9in (23cm) square

7in (18cm) zip

For the outside pocket, one piece of fabric measuring 10in (25.5cm) across by 18in (45.75cm) long

One piece of fusible fleece measuring 10 x 9in (25.5 x 23cm)

Two pieces of fabric measuring 1½in (4cm) wide by 18in (45.75cm) long

Two pieces of fusible fleece measuring 1½ x 9in (4 x 23cm)

Two 10in (25.5cm) zips

For the flap, two pieces of fabric measuring 10in (25.5cm) wide by 4½in (11.5cm) deep

One piece of fusible fleece measuring 10 x 4½in (25.5 x 11.5cm)

Large snap fastener

For the base, one piece of outer fabric measuring 12 x 5in (30.5 x 13cm)

One lining piece measuring 12 x 5in (30.5 x 13cm)

One fusible fleece measuring 12 x 5in (30.5 x 13cm)

One piece of mesh bag base measuring 11 x 4in (28 x 10cm)

190in (483cm) of 1in (2.5cm) bias binding

70in (178cm) of 1in (2.5cm) wide webbing for the strap

Two 1in (1.5cm) rectangular metal sliders

Four 1in (2.5cm) metal rectangular rings

A 10in (25.5cm) plate and a regular-sized mug to use as templates

Erasable ink pen

Clear fabric glue

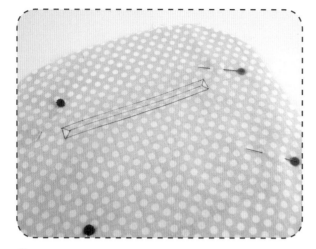

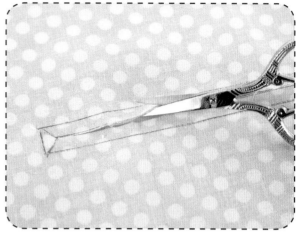

2 Take one of the lining pieces. Draw a box on the wrong side, 6in (15.25cm) long and ½in (1cm) wide, centrally, 3½in (9cm) from the top of the fabric. Draw a line through the centre, making a 'Y' shape at each end. Place one of the pocket lining pieces behind this box, so that the fabrics are right sides together.

3 Sew around the box, through both layers of fabric. Take a small pair of scissors and cut along the centre line, and carefully into the corners, taking care not to cut through the stitches.

5 Pin the 7in (18cm) zip behind the hole, then hand tack (baste) in place, before sewing with the zipper foot on your machine.

6 Place the second piece of pocket lining over the back of the zip, right side down, and sew the two pieces together. You'll need to move the main bag fabric out of the way as you sew.

7 This is how your finished inside pocket should look.

4 Push the lining fabric through the hole and press, keeping your stitched rectangle as neat and square as possible.

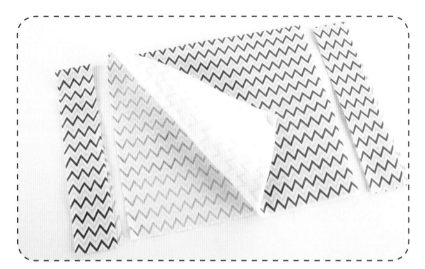

8 For the front zipped flap, fold the three long strips in half and press. Iron the fusible fleece to one half of each piece. Place the three pieces side by side, the large one in the middle, and you'll start to see how the pocket is going to be constructed.

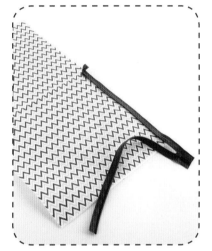

9 Open out the large middle section. Sew the first 10in (25.5cm) zip to one side, slider side down, starting in the centre crease mark of the fabric – you can sew either the backed or unbacked half as the fleece is easy to sew through. Tuck the end of the zip tape over to make neat.

10 Sew the second zip to the opposite side in the same way. Now fold the fabric over, and sew along the same stitch lines.

11 Turn right side out and press. Top-stitch alongside the zips.

12 Repeat with the second half of the zips, sandwiching them in between the long strips of fabric.

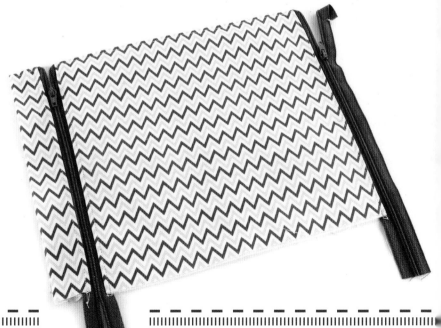

13 Mark the centre point of the pocket, 2in (5cm) down from the top, and hand sew one half of the snap fastener in place. Trim away any excess zip and put the zipped piece to one side.

14 Take the front outer piece of the bag and the strip of elastic and sew the elastic centrally and horizontally 7in (18cm) up from the bottom of the bag, making loops to hold the pens as you go (see page 43 for the finished effect, and see page 31 for the technique for creating the loops). Position the zipped pocket on top of the outer fabric for the front of the bag and sew close to the side and bottom raw edges to hold it in place.

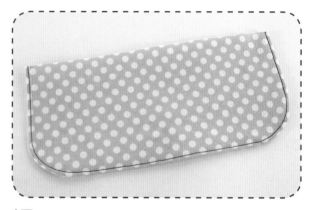

15 Iron the fusible fleece to the back of one piece of flap fabric. Then, using the cup as a template, draw then cut around the two bottom corners of both.

16 Sew the second half of the snap fastener centrally to the right side of one of the pieces, 1½in (4cm) up from the curved edge.

17 Sew the two pieces right sides together, leaving the straight top side open. Turn right side out and press. Top-stitch around the seam.

18 Sew a piece of bias tape across the top, folding the ends in to make neat. See page 15.

19 Snap together the two sides of the snap fastener, and pin, then top-stitch, the flap into position.

20 To make up the zipped panel, iron the fusible fleece to the outer two pieces of fabric. Place the 30in (76.25cm) zip slider side down over the right side of one piece, and sew the edges together.

21 Sew the second strip of unbacked fabric to the opposite side. Fold open and press. Top-stitch alongside the zip.

22 Repeat with the opposite side of the zip. Take the four 5 x 4½in (13 x 11.5cm) squares, and fuse the fleece to the two outer sides.

23 Sew one of the pieces with the fleece right sides together to the end of the zipped panel, then turn over and sew the second unbacked piece of fabric to the opposite side, so that the zipped panel is sandwiched in between them.

24 Repeat with the opposite end of the zipped panel. Press the sections, and top-stitch across the seam. Fold the panel in half and mark the centre point with erasable ink.

25 Cut four pieces from the webbing, each measuring 2½in (6.5cm) in length. Thread each one through a rectangular ring. Sew one at either side of the back bag panel, 2in (5cm) from the bottom, and two to the top, 2in (5cm) either side of the centre. Mark the top centre point with erasable ink.

26 Cut the remaining webbing in half. Take one end of each piece and thread it through the centre of a slider. Fold over and sew. Here's a tip... if you find the webbing frays, burn the ends carefully over a candle – this will melt the fabric and seal it.

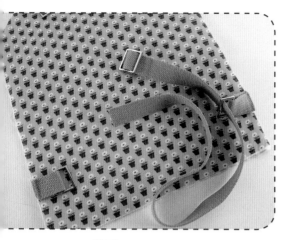

27 Thread one piece of webbing through one of the side rings.

28 Take the webbing back through the slider.

29 Then take the webbing through the top ring, being careful to make sure it is not twisting,

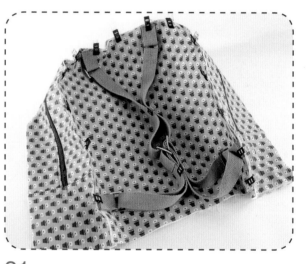

30 Fold over the end of the webbing and sew it in place. Repeat with the other strap.

31 Match the centre point of the bag to the centre point of the zipped panel and pin together; clip if your fabric is too thick to pin.

32 Sew the pieces wrong sides together, then trim away any extra length of the zipped panel. Trim the raw edge with bias binding (see page 15).

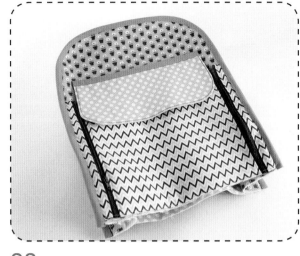

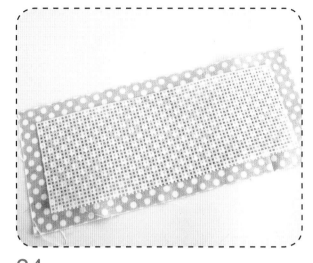

33 Sew the front of the bag to the opposite side of the zipped panel in the same way, and trim with bias binding as before.

34 Iron fusible fleece to the wrong side of the outer base fabric. Adhere the grid base to the wrong side of the base lining with a little fabric glue.

35 Place the two pieces wrong sides together, then clip or pin to the base of the bag.

36 Sew all the way round the base, then trim the raw edge with bias binding.

37 Fill the backpack with pencils and papers and you're good to get crafting!

Monkey skittles

I'm sure kids of all ages will have fun knocking down these playful, goofy monkeys – just make sure they use a fabric ball (see pages 52–53)! If you are giving these to very young children, stitch the eyes rather than using googly ones.

What you need

For each monkey:

Two pieces of dark felt measuring 6 x 9in (15.25 x 23cm)

A 4in (10cm) circle template and a 6in (15.25cm) circle template – I used plates

8 x 4in (20.5 x 10cm) light brown felt for the face, ears and tummy

2 x 3½in (5 x 9cm) bright felt for the bow tie

Two googly eyes

Toy filling

A pebble or bag of rice as a weight

Repositionable spray adhesive

Strong fabric glue

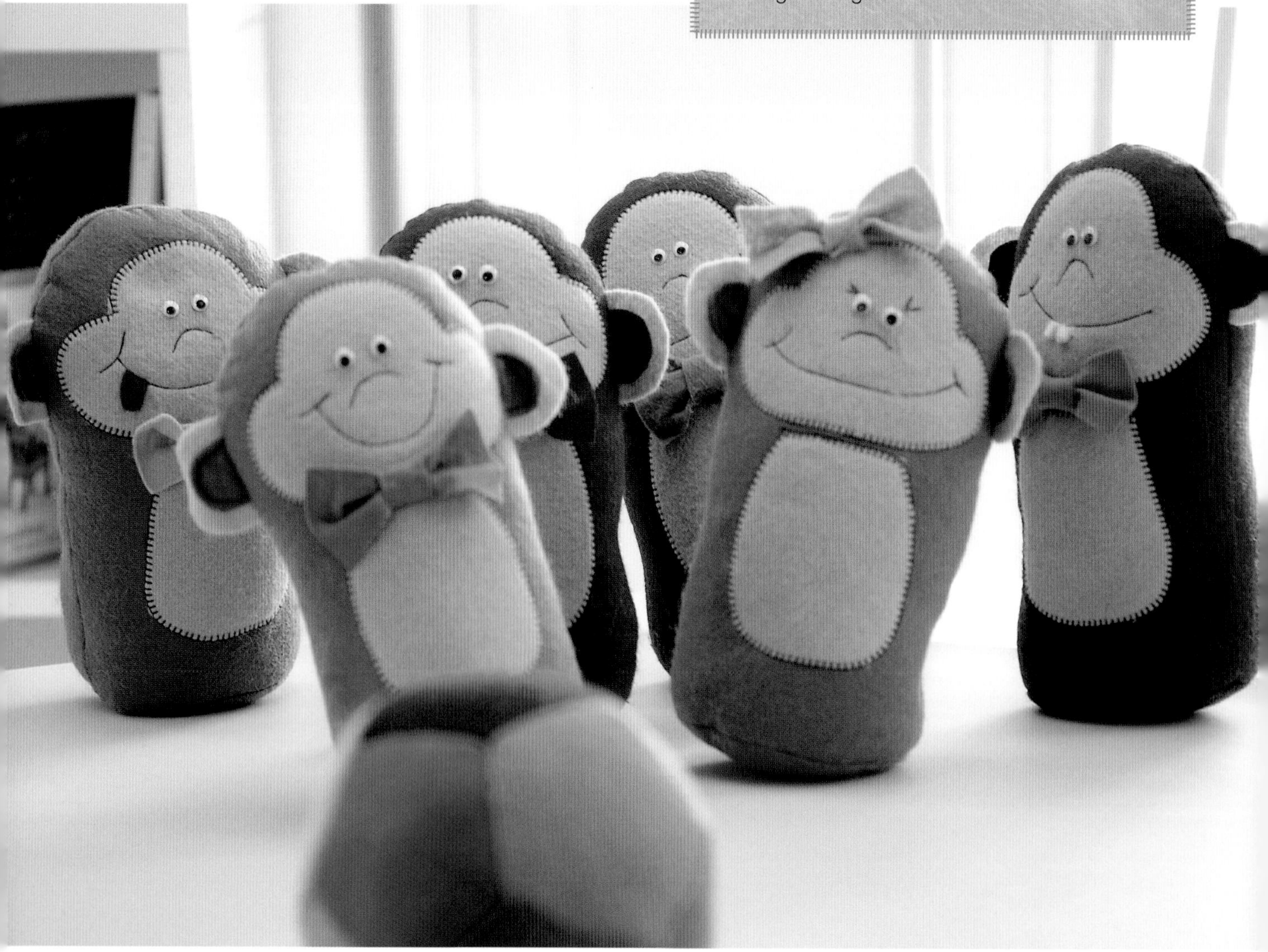

1 Take the two rectangles of felt, and using the 6in (15.25cm) template, mark then cut a curve across the top of both.

2 Cut out the face, ears and tummy using the templates on page 96. Spray the back of the face and tummy pieces with a little adhesive. Place in position on one side of the dark felt.

3 Using a small blanket stitch on your machine, or by hand, sew the face and tummy pieces in place. Start and end your stitch line under the chin – this way it doesn't matter if the stitches don't meet neatly as the bow tie will cover them.

4 Glue and then sew the dark piece of each ear inside the larger light ear pieces.

5 Draw a mouth and nose on to the monkey's face. Try to make each monkey a little different. Mark where you think the googly eyes will go.

6 Triple straight stitch over the nose and mouth on your machine. Alternatively, backstitch by hand.

7 Glue the eyes in place. If you are giving these to a very young child, stitch the eyes instead.

8 Make up the bow tie by cutting one piece of felt measuring 3 x 2in (7.5 x 5cm) – use the extra ½in (1cm) width of felt to wrap around this rectangle to make a knot. Hand stitch together.

9 Hand sew the bow tie just under the monkey's chin: you could pop a little glue behind the bow tie to make it extra secure. Tack (baste) the ears, facing inwards, to each side of the head.

10 Place the back of the monkey right sides together with the front, and sew around the curved top and sides, leaving the bottom open.

11 Cut a circle of dark felt using the 4in (10cm) template.

12 Sew the circle into the base, leaving a gap of about 3in (7.5cm) for turning.

13 Turn right side out, and stuff tightly with toy filler.

14 Just before closing, push the pebble or bag of rice inside. Hand sew the opening closed.

Tip

Why not dress your monkeys with buttons and/ or bows? Or you could appliqué an initial to the monkey's tummy to make it a bit more personal...

Hot water bottle

Fleece is such a wonderful fabric to work with when sewing for kids; it is soft, cuddly and washable and doesn't fray. Perfect for this snuggly hot water bottle cover! The pocket on the front can be home for a favourite toy at sleep time, or a place to keep a nightie nice and warm before bed!

What you need

One hot water bottle – mine measures 13in (33cm) long by 7½in (19cm) across (you will need to adjust the fabric measurements if yours is different)

20 x 20in (51 x 51cm) patterned fleece

25 x 20in (63.5 x 51cm) plain fleece

A 1½in (4cm) round template – I used a ribbon spool

A pen and a piece of card to make a template, slightly larger than your hot water bottle

1 Place the hot water bottle on the card, and draw a line around it, about 1in (2.5cm) larger all round than the bottle. To make sure the template is symmetrical, fold it in half lengthways before cutting.

2 Draw two lines across the shape, one 5in (13cm) up from the bottom edge, and one 8in (20.5cm) up from the bottom edge.

3 Cut out one plain and one patterned piece of fleece from the full template.

4 Fold the template over at the bottom line, and cut out this new top shape in both patterned and plain fleece. Open up the template, and fold over at the top line, then cut out the bottom shape in patterned and plain fleece. You will have two tops, and two bottoms that overlap to make the back of the cover.

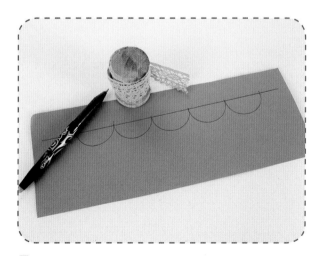

5 Cut two pieces of plain fleece for the pocket, measuring 7in (18cm) across and 6½in (16.5cm) deep.

6 Make a stencil for the scalloped trim, by drawing a 7½in (19cm) line on a piece of card, then create five semi-circles along the line by drawing around your 1½in (4cm) template.

7 Cut this scalloped shape from patterned fleece, and place over the top of one of the plain pocket pieces.

8 Sew a strip of ribbon across the straight top of the scalloped piece, attaching it to the pocket piece. Place the two pocket pieces right sides together, and sew all the way round, leaving a gap of about 3in (7.5cm) in the bottom line of stitching for turning. Snip off the corners.

9 Turn the pocket right side out and press. You may find it easier to give the fleece a light steam – try a test patch first.

10 Top-stitch across the top of the pocket, then pin it in the centre of the front of the cover and sew around the bottom three sides.

11 Take the four back pieces and, right sides together, sew across the tops of the co-ordinating pieces. Fold them over to the right sides.

12 Pin the top of the back to the top of the front, right sides together.

13 Pin on the bottom section in the same way, and sew across the bottom straight edge, as shown.

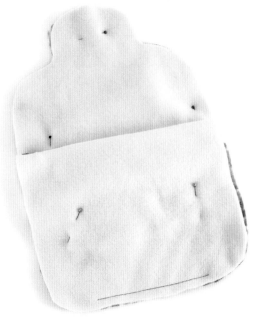

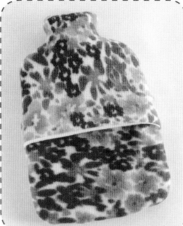

14 Place the front lining on top. Carefully remove the pins and re-pin through all the pieces of fleece. Sew all the way round apart from a gap in the bottom of about 3in (7.5cm). Snip around the curves with pinking shears.

15 Turn right side out, and hand stitch across the opening to close. The back of the cover should overlap – this is where you pop in the bottle!

Tip
You may need a little more fabric if your hot water bottle is larger than mine, but leave the pocket on the front the same size. If the cover is going to be a gift, embroider a name or initial on the pocket to make it personal!

Patchwork ball

This soft ball can be made in any size you like – I've made mine from felt but fabric would work well too.

What you need

An assortment of six different coloured felts

Toy filling

1 Cut out twelve pentagon shapes, each 3in (7.5cm) across; make two from each colour.

2 Join five pieces to one central piece by sewing with right sides facing starting ¼in (5mm) from the raw edges, and ending your stitch line ¼in (5mm) from the end.

3 Repeat with the remaining six pentagons to create a second set of joined pieces.

4 Join together the five side seams on both pieces to make them into cup shapes.

5 Sew the two halves of the ball together, right sides facing in, leaving a gap of two shapes unsewn for turning through.

6 Turn right side out and stuff tightly with toy filler.

7 Hand sew the openings closed using ladder stitch.

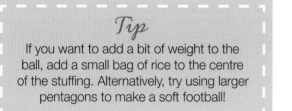

Tip

If you want to add a bit of weight to the ball, add a small bag of rice to the centre of the stuffing. Alternatively, try using larger pentagons to make a soft football!

Witch's hat

Who would have thought a witch's hat could be so pretty? I've made mine in orange felt as I thought the colour would stand out, but it would look just as good in black or green, or white for a good witch!

What you need

12in (30.5cm) square of orange felt

40 x 6in (101.5 x 15.25cm) piece of black netting

16in (40.5cm) black ribbon

Toy spider

6in (15.25cm) and 7in (18cm) circle templates – I used plates

2in (5cm) circle template – I used an egg cup

Card and pencil to make the template

Hot glue gun

Black plastic headband

A handful of toy filler

1 Draw around your 6in (15.25cm) plate onto the card to make a template. Find the centre, then draw a 2in (5cm) circle and cut it out. Cut one solid 6in (15.25cm) felt circle, and one the same size with the 2in (5cm) hole in the centre. Put these pieces to one side.

2 Draw around the 7in (18cm) plate and cut a felt circle. Cut this circle into quarters.

3 Sew the two straight edges together.

4 Turn right side out, and push this cone up through the hole in the 6in (15.25cm) circle. Hand stitch the two pieces together – you'll find this easier than machine stitching. Pop a little toy filler inside.

5 Place this section on top of the final circle, and top-stitch the two pieces together.

6 Fold the ribbon in half and hot glue the join to the back of the hat.

7 Make a bow out of the netting.

8 Hot glue to the back of the hat, on top of the ribbon.

9 Glue on the plastic spider, and any other 'witchy' embellishments you have! Glue the hat just to one side of the headband.

Pillow pal

This cute rag-doll pillow will be a favourite for years to come – she's soft and cuddly and with that cute smile is a sure winner! If you are making her for a very young child, leave out the buttons and stitch her eyes on instead..

What you need

A 16in (41cm) square pillow pad

½ yard (46cm) fabric for the cover

10in (25.5cm) square of flesh-coloured felt

10in (25.5cm) square of red felt

Four strips of fabric for the legs, each measuring 2½ x 10in (6.5 x 25.5cm)

Four strips of fabric for the arms, each measuring 2½ x 6in (6.5 x 15.25cm)

A ball of knitting yarn for the hair

Three buttons for the dress

Two small black buttons for eyes

Strong clear fabric glue

Toy filler

12 x 8in (30.5 x 20.5cm) fabric for the skirt

9in (23cm) ribbon for the belt

16in (41cm) ribbon for the shoes

16in (41cm) ribbon for the plaits

Pink alcohol ink pen to draw the cheeks

An 8in (20.5cm) round template

12in (30.5cm) zip

Erasable ink pen

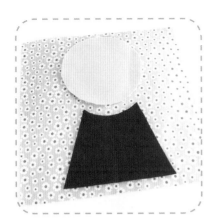

1 Cut a 16½in (42cm) square of fabric for the front of the cover.

2 Using the template, cut a circle from flesh-coloured felt. Taper the sides of the red fabric to form a long triangle. Use the template to trim the length to about 7in (18cm); arrange the pieces on your fabric to make sure they fit together as a head and dress.

3 Spray the back of the flesh-coloured circle with adhesive, and stick it in place 2½in (6.5cm) from the top. Stitch around the edge either by hand or machine – I've used a blanket stitch on my sewing machine.

4 Cut a bunch of yarn for the hair – you'll need about sixty lengths of 20in (51cm). Place over the centre top of the face. Sew across the middle of all the yarn several times to secure.

5 Loosely plait the yarn and tie with a ribbon. To make the yarn really secure, I've popped some strong fabric glue behind the plaits, then sewed them down with another length of yarn.

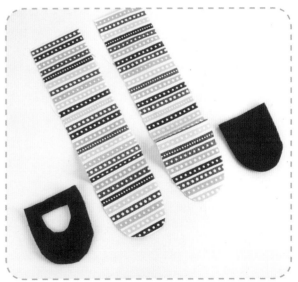

6 Mark two dots for eyes with your erasable ink pen – they look best about halfway down the face – then draw a big smile underneath! Backstitch the smile with red yarn, and sew the buttons on for eyes. The cheeks are swirls drawn on with an alcohol pen – when this is ironed it becomes permanent.

7 Now let's make the legs. Curve the foot end of each piece of fabric. Cut out four pieces of felt for the shoes, with the same curved shape as the end of the legs and 3in (7.5cm) long. Cut out a semi-circle from the middle of two of the pieces.

8 Place the four shoe pieces on top of the four leg ends, and top-stitch in place. The pieces with the solid felt shapes will form the backs of the legs; those with the semi-circles removed are the front.

9 Sew each set of leg pieces together, right sides facing, leaving the top open. Turn right side out and fill with a little toy filler, leaving the top 1in (2.5cm) unstuffed. Sew on a couple of bows to the shoes.

10 For the arms, curve the ends of the fabric strips as you did for the legs, then cut four pieces of flesh-coloured fabric for the hands, to the same curve as the fabric and 2in (5cm) long. Top-stitch to the ends of the arm pieces.

11 Sew each set of arm pieces right sides together, leaving the top open. Turn right side out and stuff with toy filler, leaving the top 1in (2.5cm) unstuffed.

12 Draw three lines on the felt with erasable ink to make fingers, then top-stitch.

13 Fold the skirt fabric in half lengthways and sew all the way round, leaving a gap in the long side of about 3in (7.5cm) for turning. Turn right side out and press. Top-stitch along one long side.

14 Using a running stitch, hand sew across the remaining long side and pull the thread to gather the fabric. You will need to gather the skirt to the width of the red felt dress, so that it covers the bottom of the dress and overhangs it by about 1in (2.5cm).

15 Tack (baste) the skirt in place, then sew the belt ribbon over the gathers. Hand sew three buttons to the front of the dress.

16 Place the dress underneath the head and pin. Push the legs under the bottom end of the felt dress and sew straight across, moving the gathered skirt out of the way as you sew.

17 Push the arms under the red felt either side of the body and pin in place. Sew down both sides of both dress and skirt, and around the neck, using a blanket stitch on your machine.

Tip

When sewing along the sides of the skirt, stop sewing about 1in (2.5cm) from the bottom to allow for the seam allowance on the pillow cover.

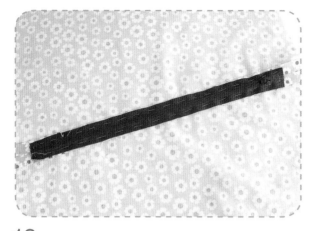

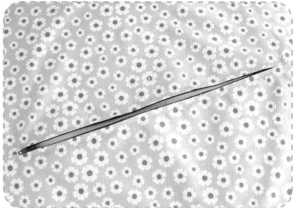

18 For the back of the pillow, cut two rectangles of fabric, each measuring 16 x 17in (41 x 43.25cm).

19 Sew together the two longer sides, right sides together, with a ½in (1cm) seam allowance. Press the seam open, pin the zip face down over the top and hand tack (baste) in place. Remove the pins.

20 With the zipper foot on your machine, sew all the way round the zip. Take your quick unpick and undo the stitches over the zip.

21 With the zip open, place the back and front of the pillow cover right sides together, tucking the legs and arms carefully inside. Sew all the way around, with a ½in (1cm) seam allowance.

22 Snip across the corners and turn the cover right side out. Push the pillow pad inside.

Tip

Why not try making different characters? My pirate was made in just the same way, but I added square felt buckles to the shoes instead of ribbon, a strip of striped fabric across the bottom of the body for his legs and a felt belt and buckle over the waist. The waistcoat is simple: two pieces of felt cut to the same shape as the body. I used shorter strands of yarn for hair and tucked them underneath a semi-circular felt hat. The dots of stubble on his chin are made with an alcohol ink pen and then ironed.

Cube tidy

This is a really quick and simple project, which can be made in any size of square. It's a great way to encourage your kids to keep their toys tidy!

What you need

Two 18in (45.75cm) squares of fabric
Foam stabiliser measuring 18in (45.75cm) square
Repositionable spray fabric adhesive
Hole punch and eight grommets
75in (190.5cm) of 1in (2.5cm) wide bias binding
Erasable ink pen

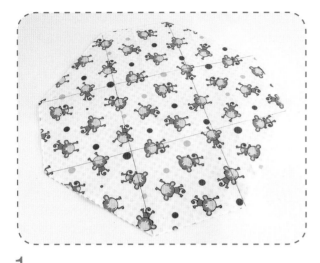

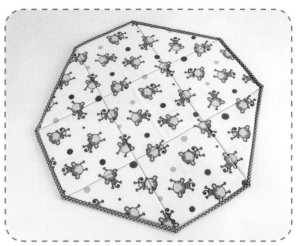

1 Using your erasable ink pen, divide one piece of fabric into nine 6in (15.25cm) squares. Cut across the corners.

2 Spray the foam with adhesive, one side at a time, and sandwich it in between the two layers of fabric.

3 Apply the bias tape all around the edge.

4 Sew along each of the marked lines.

5 Measure the centre of each triangular section, and mark a dot ½in (1cm) either side of the centre, ½in (1cm) from the bottom of the bias tape. Punch holes over these marks; these are where your grommets will be, as shown. Read the manufacturer's instructions before punching your holes and fitting the grommets.

6 Lift up the four sides of the box, with the punched triangular sections facing outwards and hold with fabric clips.

7 Thread a piece of ribbon through the holes and tie in bows to complete.

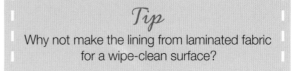

Tip
Why not make the lining from laminated fabric for a wipe-clean surface?

Chair pockets

When you're short on space for storage, what better place to keep your favourite things to hand than the side of your chair? And to top that, these chair pockets provide a comfy padded seat too!

1 Place the two smaller pieces of wadding (batting) on top of each other, over the centre of the long piece of wadding (batting), on top of one long strip of fabric, right side facing down. This will make the padded seat. Put to one side.

2 To make the contrast pockets, pin the fabric pieces wrong sides together and apply a strip of bias tape along the top edge. Remove the pins.

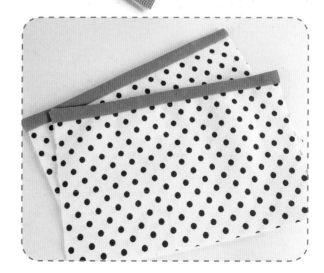

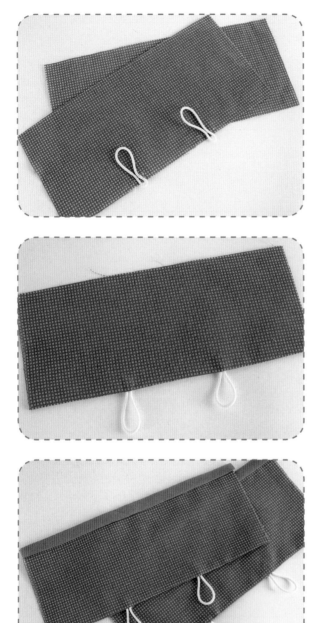

3 For the smaller pockets, first tack (baste) the hair elastics, facing inwards, to the bottom of two of the pieces, 3in (7.5cm) from the outer edges.

4 Place the remaining pocket fabric pieces over the top, right sides together, and sew across the bottom, sandwiching the elastics in between the two pieces. Turn right side out and press.

5 Apply a strip of bias binding to the top of the two smaller pockets.

6 Place then clip a contrast pocket to each end of the long piece of fabric, 2in (5cm) from the bottom. Place the pocket with hair bands over the top, aligning the bottom edges. Sew straight across the bottom of the pockets.

7 Tack (baste) along the sides of the pockets, close to the raw edge.

8 Place this whole section wrong sides together with the fabric and wadding (batting) layers created in step 1, and pin in position. Sew bias tape all around the edge, making sure you fold the hair elastics out of the way so that they are not trapped in the seam.

Tip

If you want to stop the pocket from slipping on the chair, pop a few dots of silicone glue on the underside and leave to dry.

Porthole curtains

This fun curtain easily disguises messy shelves, but made on a larger scale it could fit in the recess of a window to create a pirate captain's cabin.

What you need

½ yard (46cm) of striped canvas fabric

An 8in (20.5cm) circle template

Erasable ink pen

Three 9in (23cm) circles of clear vinyl

An extending curtain pole that fits inside the recess

60in (152.5cm) of ¼in (5mm) wide piping cord

60in (152.5cm) of 1in (2.5cm) bias binding

18in (45.75cm) of ribbon cut into three 6in (15.25cm) strips

Hot glue gun

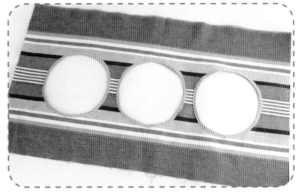

1 Draw around your template with your erasable ink pen, spacing three circles evenly across the centre of the fabric, as shown. Cut out the circles.

2 Apply the bias binding around the holes. I found it easiest to fold and press the tape in half lengthways first, wrap the tape around the raw edge of the hole and then sew both sides at the same time.

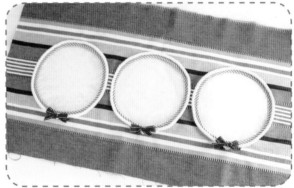

3 Pop a little hot glue around the holes on the wrong side and lay the vinyl circles over the top, one at a time. If your vinyl is creased, lightly press with a piece of fabric over the vinyl, then leave to cool before moving.

4 From the right side, and starting from the bottom of the holes, glue around the outside of the bias tape and add the piping cord. To cover the joins, add a bow at the base of each window.

5 Fold over the sides and bottom of the curtain twice by ½in (1cm) to make a hem, and sew. Fold the top over by ¼in (5mm) then 1in (2.5cm). Press. Sew along the folded edge to make a channel to thread the curtain pole through.

6 Insert the pole into the channel and you're ready to hang!

71

Pyjama eater

What a great way to teach your kids to keep their room tidy! This quirky monster will hang on the back of the door and gobble up anything from pyjamas to laundry – or why not make larger monsters to store toys?

What you need

½ yard (46cm) fabric

Child's coat hanger – mine is 10in (25.5cm) wide, so I cut my fabric to 1in (2.5cm) wider than this. Adapt your own fabric as necessary

¼ yard (23cm) fusible fleece

Scraps of white, black, red and yellow felt

Repositionable spray adhesive

Erasable ink pen

1 Cut the fabric into four 11 x 18in (28 x 46cm) strips. Fuse the fleece to the wrong sides of two of the fabric pieces. Place the coat hanger at the top of one piece, and follow the curve of the coat hanger to draw an arc with your erasable ink pen. Cut around this arc, then use this piece as a template to shape the other three pieces.

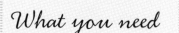

2 Take one of the pieces of fabric with fleece backing and one without, place right sides together, and cut a curve straight across both, slightly above halfway.

3 Cut two different sized circles from white felt for the eyes: mine measure 2in (5cm) and 3in (7.5cm) across. Cut two small black circles for pupils. The teeth are two rectangles measuring about 1 x 1½in (2.5 x 4cm). Cut the tongue about 5in (13cm) long. The yellow felt hair is simply a zigzag cut, then shaped, to the top of the head.

4 Use the cut pieces of fabric that are backed with fleece. Spray a little repositionable adhesive to the eyes and pop them in place, then do the same with the black felt pupils – the monster face looks quite funny with the eyes looking in different directions! Sew the eyes in place with a blanket stitch on your machine, or by hand if you prefer.

5 Sew along the top edge of the tongue, positioning it so that it faces downwards, stitching close to the edge, and do the same with the teeth, facing upwards.

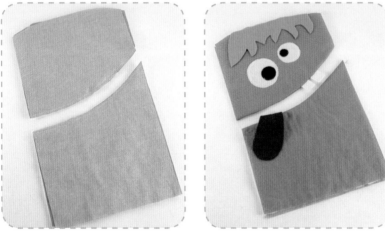

6 Place the remaining pieces of cut fabric right sides together with the face, and sew across the curved edges of both.

7 Turn over and press.

8 Take the second piece of fabric that is backed with fleece, and place the 'chin' of the monster over the top, right side facing down. Sew straight across the bottom.

9 Place the top of the face right sides together over the top of this section – there will be a gap of about 1in (2.5cm) between the two face pieces – this forms the mouth. The final large piece of fabric goes on top, right sides together. Pin. Mark the centre point at the top. Sew all the way around, leaving a gap in the bottom of about 4in (10cm) for turning, and a gap in the top centre of ½in (1cm) for the hanger.

10 Turn right side out, then sew the opening in the lining closed. Press. Push the hanger through the top hole and your pyjama eater is ready to do his job!

Tip
Try making a few monsters with different expressions for fun bedroom storage!

Shoe bag

Ideal for storing shoes at home or taking them to school, this simple-to-make drawstring bag is so versatile! A gift bag, toy bag or book bag – I'm sure everyone will find a use for it.

What you need

One piece of outer fabric measuring 14in (35.5cm) wide by 20in (51cm) deep

One piece of lining measuring 15 x 20in (38 x 51cm)

Two small pieces of tear-away stabiliser

30in (76cm) cord

Erasable ink pen

Button hole foot for your sewing machine

Safety pin

1 Draw a line with your erasable ink pen 1½in (4cm) from the top of the outer fabric, then another ¾in (2cm) under this. This will be the channel where the cord is threaded. Mark another line, ¾in (2cm) from each end of this channel. Sew a buttonhole at this point (I sewed mine with orange thread): pop a piece of tear-away stabiliser behind before you stitch to help keep the fabric in shape. If you don't have a buttonhole stitch on your sewing machine, you could use an eyelet punch instead.

2 Sew the top of the outer fabric to the top of the lining fabric, right sides together. Open it out.

3 Fold the piece in half lengthways, then sew the whole length of the bag, making sure that the edges of the seam you've just sewn meet neatly.

4 Fold this tube so that the seam is in the centre, and sew across the bottom of the outer fabric. Then sew across the lining, but leave a gap of about 4in (10cm) for turning.

5 Pinch the bottom seam with your fingers so that it sits on top of the side of the bag. Sew across each corner, 1in (2.5cm) from the point, to create a square base. Do this for both the lining and the outer fabric.

6 Turn right side out. Sew across the opening in the lining on your machine. Push the lining inside the bag. As the lining was cut 1in (2.5cm) longer it will form a border around the top of the bag.

7 Top-stitch around the seam – you will find it easier to use the free arm on your sewing machine. Now top-stitch around the two marked channel lines.

8 Thread the cord on to a safety pin and thread through one of the buttonholes, round the channel and out through the other buttonhole.

9 Knot the two ends of the string together.

Tip
When sewing buttonholes, I always stitch them first on a scrap piece of fabric so that I know they'll be the right size.

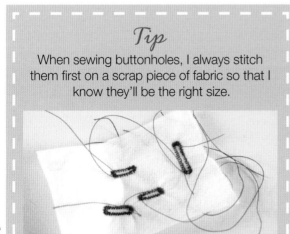

Roaring storing!

Take a pencil or pen from the lion's mouth if you dare! This zippered pouch can be made in any size you like, to make anything from a small coin purse to a pyjama case.

What you need

Two circles of orange fabric and two circles of red fabric measuring 8in (20.5cm) across

Two circles of fusible fleece measuring 8in (20.5cm) across

A 9in (23cm) white nylon zip

Four triangles of orange fabric for the ears measuring 3in (7.5cm) tall and 3in (7.5cm) across the bottom, with curved sides

Two pieces of fusible fleece cut to the same shape as the ears

Cream yarn for the mane

A 1½in (4cm) triangle of black felt for the nose

Two buttons for eyes

Black embroidery thread

White embroidery thread

Erasable ink pen

Tacking glue stick

1 Fuse the fleece to the wrong sides of the orange circles and two of the ear pieces.

2 Take one orange circle and draw a line 3in (7.5cm) from one edge with your erasable ink pen (this will form the mouth). Then draw a triangle for the nose and a couple of small circles where the eyes will be. Already it's starting to look like a cat!

3 Cut across the mouth.

4 Take one of the red circles and cut across the same line.

5 Sew the top edge of the 'mouth' to the top of the zip, then sew the bottom edge of the mouth to the opposite side of the zip.

6 Sew on the buttons for eyes: I've used black buttons with white embroidery thread, as it gives the eyes a lifelike look. Sew on the black felt triangular nose, and hand embroider a line from the nose to the zip in black thread.

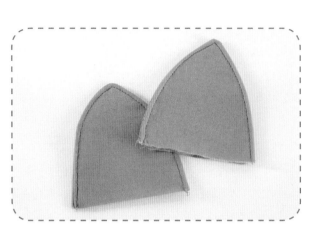

7 Sew the red lining pieces to the opposite side of the zip tape, so that the zip is sandwiched in between two pieces of fabric. Trim away the excess zip, and hand-sew the open end of the zip together. Top-stitch either side of the zip.

8 Sew the ear pieces right sides together, one piece of ear fused with fleece with one piece without, just around the top two sides. Snip across the top of the ear, then turn right side out and press. Top-stitch.

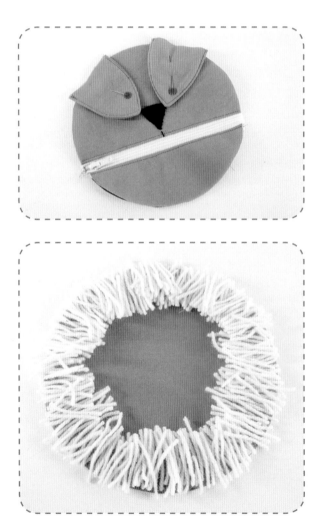

9 Pin to the top front of the head, facing inwards.

10 Sew the ears in place and remove the pins.

11 Cut the yarn into 2in (5cm) lengths, by winding it around two of your fingers, then cutting it in half. Glue around the edge of the second circle with tacking glue and lay the pieces of yarn evenly around the edge of the circle, facing inwards.

12 Place the 'face' of the lion right side down over this fringed side, and sew all the way around. Make sure the zip is open as you'll need to turn the pouch through the opening.

13 Now place the remaining red circle over the top of the sewn red circle, and sew through all layers, leaving a gap in the bottom of about 3in (7.5cm) for turning.

14 Turn through the lining and hand stitch the opening closed. Then turn again through the zip to reveal a fierce lion face! Press, and trim the mane to make it neat if needed.

Tip
You could add a loop of ribbon to the back of the head and hang this on the wall or the end of the bed, or make a smaller face with a ribbon to use as a wristlet.

Kite wall hanging

This colourful kite will brighten up any child's bedroom, with the tail making a fun place to peg pictures and notes.

What you need

Two mirror-imaged right-angled triangles of fabric measuring 18in (46cm) long by 10in (25.5cm) across: I used two different prints

Two mirror imaged right-angled triangles of fabric measuring 13in (33cm) long by 10in (25.5cm) across: I used two different prints

For the lining, a piece of fabric measuring 31 x 20in (78.75 x 51cm) – you may need to join two pieces to make this size

31 x 20in (78.75 x 51cm) fusible fleece

60in (152.5cm) of 1in (2.5cm) wide stiff interfacing

12in (30.5cm) of ¼in (5mm) wide ribbon

30in (76cm) of ½in (1cm) ribbon for the small bows

12in (30.5cm) of 1in (2.5cm) wide ribbon for the large bow

Five curtain rings

Craft pegs

Fabric glue

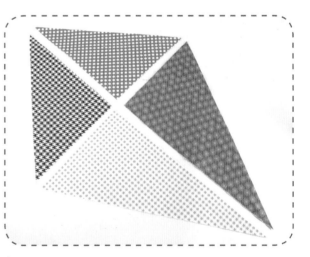

1 Arrange the four triangles in the shape of a kite.

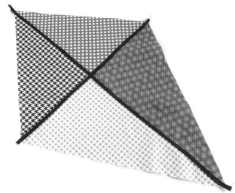

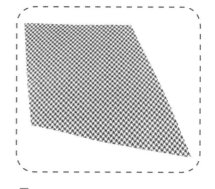

2 Sew one small triangle to one large triangle, right sides together, then repeat with the remaining two. Press, then sew these two pieces together straight down the centre. Sew strips of ¼in (5mm) wide ribbon over the seams.

3 Fuse the fleece to the back of the kite and trim to the same size.

4 Cut the stiff interfacing into strips and glue to the fleece side of the kite to help strengthen it, as shown above.

5 Use this kite shape as a template to cut the lining.

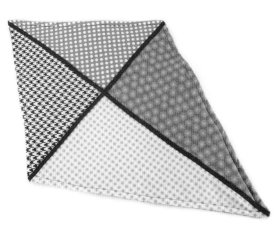

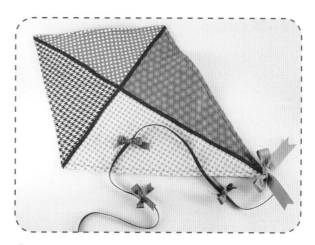

6 Sew the lining and the kite fabric pieces right sides together, leaving a gap of about 5in (13cm) in one side for turning.

7 Turn right side out and press, then top-stitch all the way around.

8 Hand sew the remaining ¼in (5mm) ribbon to the base of the kite to form a tail, and cover the join with a bow made from 1in (2.5cm) wide ribbon. You can either hand stitch or glue this in place.

9 Make small bows from the ½in (1cm) wide ribbon, and sew along the tail.

10 Sew one curtain hook to the top lining side of the kite by hand, then another to the right corner of the lining, and two along the tail, depending on how you'd like it to hang. To decide, offer the kite up to the wall, and pop a pin into the points it will hang from.

11 Hang on the wall with small tacks, then peg pictures onto the tail!

Caravan caddy

This little play caravan is for a girl on the go! Use it as a portable doll's house, or as storage for pens and paper.

What you need

Two pieces of fabric, 14 x 6in (35.5 x 15.25cm), for the top half of the caravan

Two pieces of striped fabric, 14 x 4in (35.5 x 10cm) for the bottom half of the caravan

Two pieces of foam stabiliser, 14 x 9in (35.5 x 23cm)

For the base, two pieces of fabric and one of foam stabiliser, 14 x 1½in (35.5 x 4cm)

76in (193cm) of 1in (2.5cm) wide bias binding

For the door, two pieces of fabric, 4 x 7in (10 x 18cm)

White fabric for the door's window, 2 x 3in (5 x 7.5cm)

Small button for the door handle

1in (2.5cm) strip of hook and loop fastening

For the inside door, one piece of white fabric, 3 x 5in (7.5 x 13cm)

A piece of ¼in (5mm) elastic, 3in (7.5cm) long

White fabric for the window, 4 x 3in (10 x 7.5cm)

The curtains are two pieces of fabric measuring 4 x 3in (10 x 7.5cm)

Two small buttons to pin the curtains back

Floral fabric scraps for the flowers and grass

The bunting is made up of twelve 1½in (4cm) long triangles of fabric

One elastic hair band

Two contrasting buttons and embroidery thread to fasten the caddy

Two strips of 1in (2.5cm) wide webbing for the handles, each 12in (30.5cm) long

Repositionable spray adhesive

10in (25.5cm) and 4in (10cm) circle templates

Erasable ink pen – I prefer heat-erasable

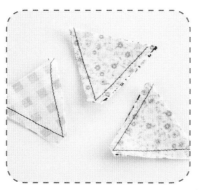

1 Cut out twelve triangles for the bunting, 1½in (4cm) across and 1½in (4cm) long. Sew them, right sides together, in pairs. Snip across the points. Turn right side out and press.

2 For the outside of the caravan, sew together the top and bottom pieces of fabric, right sides together, then press. Top-stitch along the seam. Repeat with the remaining two pieces so you have a front and back to the caravan.

3 Spray the reverse of both the front and back pieces of the caravan and place on top of the foam stabiliser pieces. Using your large circle template, round off the top two corners of each.

4 On both the front and back pieces, use your erasable ink pen to draw lines across the width of the top part of the caravan, 1in (2.5cm) apart, then straight stitch over the lines to look like panels on the caravan. Put the back of the caravan to one side.

5 Now make up the door. Cut a curve at the top of the door fabric and its window fabric, using the small circle template. Also cut a curved top to the back of the door piece and put to one side. Adhere the window to the front of the door, and satin stitch all the way round. Draw a cross in the centre of the window with erasable ink, and satin stitch over the top. Sew the small button to the left-hand side.

6 Sew one half of the hook and loop fastening halfway down the right side of the back of the door, ½in (1cm) from the right-hand edge. Sew the two door pieces right sides together, leaving the bottom open for turning. Turn right side out and press, folding the open end inwards by ¼in (5mm).

7 Top-stitch all the way round.

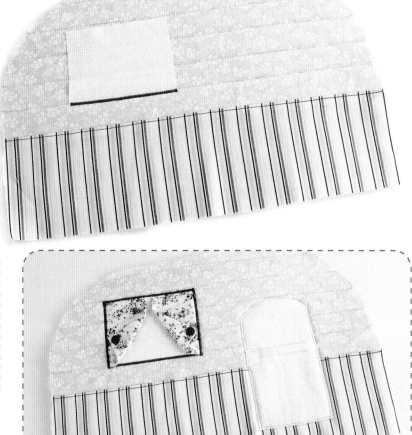

8 Place the window to the left-hand side of the caravan front, as shown, and adhere with repositionable adhesive. Satin stitch across the bottom edge.

9 To make the curtains, fold the two pieces of fabric in half, right sides together, and sew across the bottom edges. Turn right side out and press.

10 Place the curtains over the window, with the sewn edges at the bottom, and satin stitch around the three top sides. Fold back the curtains and secure by hand sewing on the two small buttons.

11 Take the white inside door, and curve the top with your 4in (10cm) template. Adhere this to the right of the window, place the piece of elastic across the door about halfway down, and satin stitch all the way round, trapping the elastic as you sew. The remaining piece of hook and loop fastening is sewn to the left side of the inner door – align it correctly using the hook and loop fastening on the back of the door.

12 Place the door over the top of the inside door, making sure the hook and loop fastening meets, and sew down the right-hand side.

13 Draw a wavy line with your erasable ink pen across the top of your caravan, no closer to the edge than 1in (2.5cm) to allow for the seam. Spray the back of your pennants with repositionable spray and stick in place. Be careful not to overlap the door!

14 Sew across your drawn line – I've used a pin stitch on my sewing machine – and catch the tops of the pennants to hold them in place.

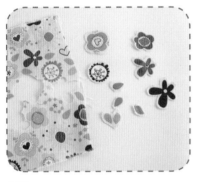

15 Cut out a few flowers and leaves from your printed fabric, along with a small strip of grass.

16 Arrange these under the window and sew either by hand or machine.

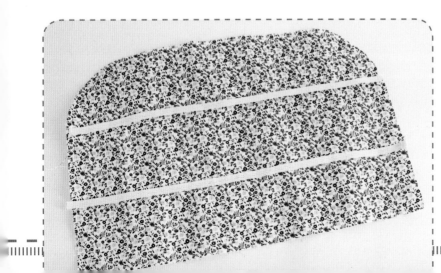

17 Cut the elastic into four strips and pin two to each lining piece of fabric; space them about 3in (7.5cm) apart. Sew at intervals of your choice to create little loops to hold the toys.

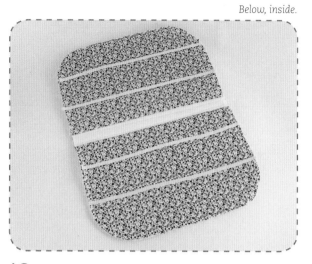

Left, outside.

Below, inside.

18 Place a lining piece right sides together with each of the outer pieces, and machine stitch along the long, straight edge of each pair. Open out and fold back so that the fabrics now sit with the wrong sides facing. Machine stitch one side of a piece of bias binding across the bottom of the back caravan piece.

19 Adhere the base piece of foam stabiliser in between the two base strips of fabric with spray adhesive. Place this under the bias binding at the bottom of the back panel and top-stitch. Sew another piece of bias binding to the bottom of the front panel, then top-stitch to the base, so that you create a 'hinge' joining the front and back together at the base.

20 Take the back section of the caravan, and work only with the outer layer of fabric. Fold the top edge in half to crease the centre point, and hand stitch the hair elastic facing inwards at the top point.

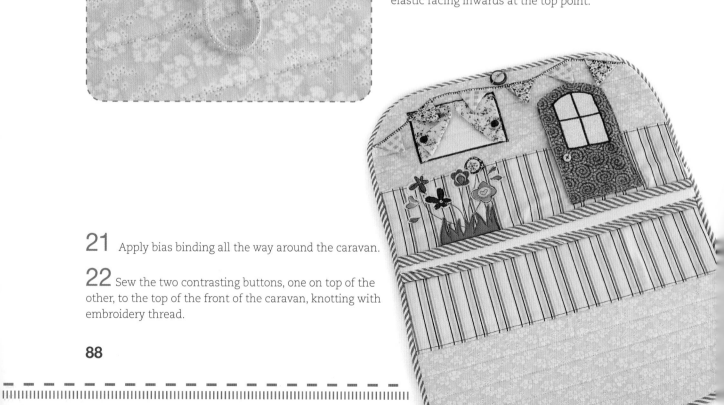

21 Apply bias binding all the way around the caravan.

22 Sew the two contrasting buttons, one on top of the other, to the top of the front of the caravan, knotting with embroidery thread.

23 Measure 2in (5cm) either side of the button fastening and sew one webbing handle on here. Fold the caddy together and mark the position of the second handle on the back side. Sew in place.

24 Ready to play?

Tip
You could make the caravan extra special by printing a photograph onto printable cotton and popping it into the window!

Miss Monster bookend

Here's a monster who's really not scary at all – she'll happily keep your books in place, or even prop a door open! Her mouth makes a handy pocket and she likes to munch on pencils!

What you need

For the body:

Two rectangles of fabric measuring 11in (28cm) square – plain for the front and patterned for the back

Two rectangles of fabric for the mouth measuring 11 x 7in (28 x 18cm)

Three 12in (30.5cm) long chenille sticks

Toy filler

Red embroidery thread

A weight such as a pebble

A 12in (30.5cm) circle template

Erasable ink pen

A red alcohol ink pen

For the eyes:

Two small black buttons

Two circles of white felt measuring ½in (1cm) across

Two blue circles of felt measuring 1½in (4cm) across

Two semi-circles of red felt measuring 2in (5cm) across

Two strips of black felt measuring ½ x 2in (1 x 5cm)

1 Take the two large rectangles of fabric and using the circle template, draw, then cut, a curve from the top two corners. Cut a 1½in (4cm) square from each of the bottom corners.

2 To make the mouth, place the two pieces of fabric right sides together and draw a curve across the top using the circle template, then draw a zigzag line across the curve to look like teeth. Cut along the zigzag line through both pieces of fabric.

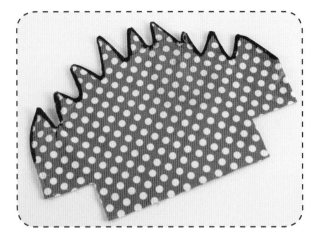

3 Sew along the zigzag edge, then turn right side out and press. Cut a 1½in (4cm) square from each bottom corner. Draw over the zigzag edge with your alcohol ink pen to make the teeth stand out – the ink in these pens becomes permanent after ironing.

4 Place the zigzag mouth piece over the bottom of the plain fabric to see how much space you have to play with, then work out the position of the eyes. Have a play with their arrangement, and expression – it's easy to create a cross or surprised look depending on how you place the eyelids!

5 When you're happy, pin everything in place and remove the mouth piece. First sew the blue circles, then the white on top, and the button on top of the white. Sew the eyelids in place, then snip a fringe into the black strips to make eyelashes. Sew these along the straight edges of the eyelids.

6 To make the scar, draw a 3in (7.5cm) line with your erasable ink pen on one side of the face, then draw ½in (1cm) lines across it to look like stitches. Hand embroider a backstitch over the lines.

7 Place the mouth section back over the face and you're ready to sew Miss Monster together!

8 Place the back of the monster right sides together with the front, sandwiching the mouth in between.

9 Sew around the top curved side, then across the bottom but leave a gap of about 3in (7.5cm) for turning. Don't sew the cut-out corners at this stage.

10 Open out the corners so that the side seams sit over the bottom seam, and sew straight across to make the base square (see also page 14).

11 Turn right side out, and stuff tightly with toy filler. Push your weight into the bottom before hand stitching the opening closed.

12 Bend the chenille sticks in half, and hand sew them to the centre top of the head. Wrap them around your finger to make spirals to complete.

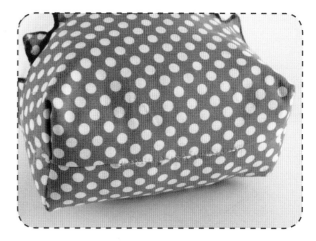

Tip

If you're making a pair of bookends, try experimenting with different expressions: add a nose and ears, or maybe Miss Monster would like a Mister Monster friend?

Coin purse

This is a really simple-to-make purse – pocket money will be kept safe as the purse can hook onto a belt loop or bag. I've made this from wipe-clean laminated fabric.

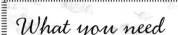

What you need

One piece of laminated fabric measuring 6 x 8in (15.25 x 20.5cm)

One piece of lining fabric measuring 6 x 8in (15.25 x 20.5cm)

24in (61cm) of continuous zip

5in (13cm) of ribbon

5in (13cm) of 1in (2.5cm) wide bias binding

One swivel snap hook

An 8in (20.5cm) circular template – I used a plate

Erasable ink pen

Tip

Try making the purse in different sizes – it's a great shape for a sunglasses case or pencil pouch!

1 Place the template over the top of both pieces of fabric, mark, then cut an arc from the top.

2 Take the slider off the zip and pull apart the two sides, you'll only use one side of the zip for this purse. Sew the zip, with the teeth facing inwards, around the curved side of the laminated fabric, leaving 2in (5cm) of zip extra at each end.

3 Place the lining on top, right sides together, and sew over the first row of stitching. Turn the purse right side out.

4 Fold over the two sides of the purse, and re-attach the slider to the zip. Do it up about 2in (5cm) to keep the fabrics securely fastened. See page 13.

5 Trim away the excess zip, and turn the purse inside out. Fold the ribbon in half, and push inside the bottom of the purse, facing inwards so that the raw edges meet with the raw edges of the purse, under the zip. Sew across the opening.

6 Apply the bias binding across this seam, folding the ends inwards to make neat. Turn right side out, and attach the latch to the slider on the zip.

Templates

Monkey's ears, face and tummy for the Monkey skittles, pages 44–47, given at actual size:

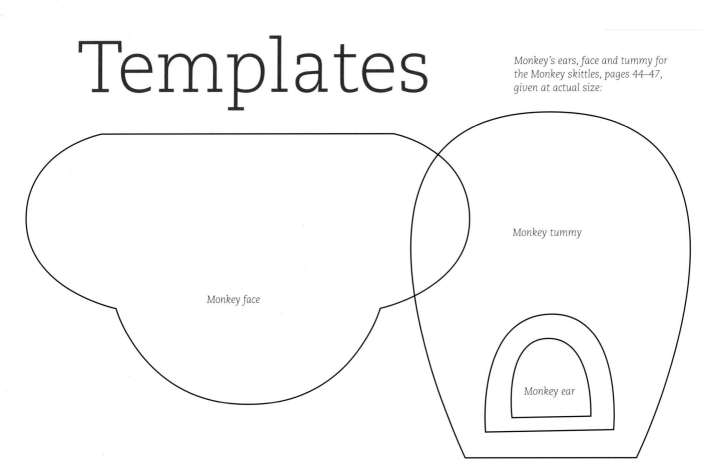

Monkey face

Monkey tummy

Monkey ear

Index